I0201157

KNOWING ELSIE…

THE INSPIRING CLARITY TO THE

SIMPLICITY OF LIFE

BY: MICHELE CAMPBELL

ISBN: 978-0-578-91690-3

Contributor:

Cameron Campbell – Picture (Cover page)

Anonymous - Editor

All rights reserved.

No permission has been granted for this book to be reproduced in it's entirety in any form. No part of this book should be reproduced or otherwise, without prior written approval from the author/publisher except for a short extract from the text for the purpose of a brief quote.

This book is a work of inspiration. Other than Elsie, the names, characters, and examples used are of the authors creation primarily to express the authors point. Any likeness to actual situations or an individual is completely by chance.

First edition, May 2021

Dedication

To Elsie,

A women who has always inspired me, awed me, and amazed me. I can't imagine growing up in a world without you in it. The simple things in life that I have learned from you has allowed me to treasure the life I have been given. I have always considered myself blessed because I have always known you. Having such a remarkable women in my life is a blessing. A lot of people have tried to put the "Hows" and "Whys" of a happy life into words. Perhaps, some individuals are born positive and happy; it's in their genetics. Or, they look at the world "through rose-colored glasses." For me... It is and always has been... Knowing Elsie...

Table of Contents

Chapter One

GIVE

CREDENCE

TO

THYSELF

Believe in yourself!

Did you know that everyone struggles with confidence at some point in their lifetime? Some people may never openly admit it, however, self-doubt is a natural state of mind for many individuals. The uncertainties that creep into the mind is an attempt to transform positive thinking into negative thoughts. These thoughts lead to self-doubt. What is self-doubt? It's described as someone having uncertainties about their own abilities and usefulness. These types of thoughts can cause an individual to feel overwhelmed. There is a difference in the anxiety level between a confident individual and someone who struggles with trusting in their own abilities. The confident individual has become mindfully self-aware. This means that they have become capable of recognizing self-doubt, therefore, they are able to overcome their own internal critic. Having trust in one's self is essential. It allows us to redirect our own reflective consciousness. Take a moment to reflect. Do you ever remember doubting yourself? Have you ever questioned your own potential? Have you ever thought that maybe you just don't have what it takes and there is no point in trying? Recognize that this is self-doubt and these are self-defeating thoughts. We all have the power to redirect these negative thoughts into positive affirmations. It's important to believe that we can accomplish anything we set our minds to accomplish. It's absolutely necessary that we maintain faith in our own abilities in order to achieve our desired objectives. Our internal-critic is often a pessimistic. It will often try to influence us to give up. Especially, if we encounter a difficult situation or we make a mistake. Our internal-critic is eager to supply us with justifications that will convince us to abandon hope. We have to challenge this way of thinking and encourage ourselves to progress forward. It helps to remind ourselves that mistakes are a natural part of life and are actually fundamental in our development. Everyone makes mistakes and everyone gets disappointed at sometime or another. Once we become mindfully aware, we can use our internal critic to reflect on our behaviors and enhance our own personal growth. We can advise ourselves on how to better respond to disheartening situations in the future. Self-reflection is healthy and it enables us to grow. Because, if we focus on the things our internal-critic has to say, it will keep us second guessing ourselves. This will avert us from reaching our full potential. It will also prevent us from unlocking the person within us that we yearn to become, our ideal self. All those negative thoughts that keep our minds busy are also responsible for creating the fear that keeps us trapped in our safe-zone. Then, all the negative bombarding begins to eat away at our motivation. We become scared to take risk, put ourselves out there, and we loose faith in our own abilities. This is NOT who we're meant to be! It can be challenging to find a comfortable level of confidence because no one wants to come across as lacking in confidence nor do they want to come across as arrogant. However, it's possible to find our own *confidence equilibrium*. This is a level of confidence that we feel comfortable with that will allow us to become our ideal selves. Everyone knows that self-esteem has a lot to do with self-confidence and how someone may perceive themselves. However, not everyone who struggles with self-confidence and self-doubt have a low self-esteem. There are a lot of self-help articles and books that focus on low self-esteem issues. Especially, related to the specific generalization of negative low self-esteem and the impact it imposes on someone's self-confidence. However, some people are not aware that many people have probably experienced situational low self-esteem or will experience it. This is described as an unfavorable self-image relating to a specific circumstance or a present situation. Have you ever felt your self-esteem fluctuate at work or school based on positive or negative feedback? One day you may leave work or school feeling like you are on top of the world. However, the very next day you may leave work or school feeling upset, stressed, and defeated. This is related to what some specialist call situational low self-esteem. There is a strong possibility that sometime during the day you may have personalized a situation or incident that caused you to respond in a negative manner which left you feeling defeated. These feelings can cause us to automatically respond in a self-destructive manner. Which can lead to a negative self-reflection based on the situation at hand. It can be difficult to control our own impulsive actions, even though we recognize that we maybe over reacting, at the time in which we are over reacting. Did you know that many people can relate to this emotional response? We're emotional creatures by nature. There are more neural fibers transmitting from the emotional parts of our brains feeding into the logical/rational center of our brains than there are coming from the logical/rational center of our brains feeding into the emotional side. We may very well say that we are indeed ruled by our emotions. When we undergo stressful situations our bodies produce a stress hormone called cortisol. This hormone creates the feelings of despair. These feelings are more prominent when a person feels like they have failed at something. This makes it difficult for the rational side of our brains to seize control over our thought process and our response system. Unfortunately, emotions are an involuntary response and not something we have learned, but everyone can learn from them. This is how we can develop a sense of self-control. We know that these self-destructive behaviors are caused by a natural state of mind which are induced by hormones that our body produces as a defense response to stress. Therefore, we need to learn to forgive ourselves in the same manner that we would forgive others. Our emotions allow us the opportunity to understand ourselves on a deeper level, if we take the time to understand them. Our emotions tell us what we want and what we don't want. Once we're able to understand our emotions, the causes and the effects, we will be more capable of controlling them by using logic and reasoning. One way to increase our skills in order to better respond in stressful situations is by increasing our meta-cognitive knowledge. This is simply to become aware of the reasons we think in the manner in which we think. In order to enhance our own knowledge, we can learn new skills and strategies. Habits and unconscious responses can be difficult to change but we can make a commitment to change. By making a commitment to change we are giving ourselves strength. The commitment needs to be strong. We need to stay away from saying, "I need to change," or "I need to stop doing that," because it's not the same as saying, "I will change," or "I will stop doing that." The affirmation or emphasis that we place on our commitment does matter. It indicates a firm decision and we are less likely to change our mind. There will be set-backs but we are capable of redirecting ourselves to maintain our goal. Especially, when we make a strong commitment to ourselves. We need to focus on the present and stay in the here-and-now. We can't allow our auto-pilot or subconscious to drive us. It will drive us on a path that we have already programmed. Therefore, we need to take the wheel, be alert, and program a new path. We need to focus on why this change is important to us (This could be family, friends, or personal success). We need to stay optimistic about our success. I have a friend that has admitted that when she gets stressed and someone raises their voice at her or makes a snide-condescending remark towards her that she has a tendency to over react. Then, she begins to feel bad (This could probably be classified as situational low self-esteem). The cortisol being released during this agitated moment contributes to her emotional state. Therefore, having this knowledge and understanding, she changed her perspective and made a commitment to herself that the next time someone raised their voice at her or spoke to her in a snide-condescending manner that she was not going to get angry. She changed her perspective to view their rudeness as a distressed emotional state that they, themselves, were experiencing. This brought upon negative emotions in them that they have not recognized or became self-aware of at this point in time. She made a commitment to herself that she wouldn't over react or judge them. She chooses to acknowledge that stress can impact everyone's actions. Therefore, she decided to show compassion and forgiveness towards their disrespect. This gives her the power to control her own emotional response to the situation. Her understanding and acceptance that the other person maybe struggling with some sort of emotional stress allows her to forgive their behavior and prevents her from over reacting. By viewing it this way, she takes less offense to their actions. She genuinely feels compassion for them because they have so much vexation about life that they would behave in such a manner. Her technique is great because it works for her. She has been able to acknowledge her own feelings, examine the situation as a whole, and change her perception to better counter act her own emotional response. She openly admits that she still looses control sometimes, but not as often as she did before she changed her perception of the situation. She has learned to forgive herself for being human and has learned to forgive the trespasses of others. Everyone makes mistakes, everyone has bad days, and emotions are part of reality. This is an example of how someone can realign their perspective to overcome a negative emotional response with a positive reaction. Personal growth can be stimulating and motivating for everyone. It can be influential in encouraging the people around us in a positive manner. There are many positive ways that we can build our confidence and strengthen our own areas of weakness. It is important that we stay humble and not cross the line of arrogance. People who are truly confident in themselves and their decisions stay open to others (they listen, take advice, and they don't act like a know-it-all). They are open to admit that they make mistakes because they are still learning. There isn't anyone in the world that knows everything. The world offers limitless information and there is always something new to be learned. It's okay for us to say, "I don't know," or "I am not sure" these are true answers. It is always best to avoid perfectionism because no body is perfect. It isn't ever a good idea to provide an answer as a fact, if we are not sure that it is true. This can lead to the spreading of misinformation. It is best to admit that we simply are ignorant or uneducated on the subject matter. We can always offer to look into it further, or suggest a viable source to obtain the information, if someone needs assistance. We don't have to be the best in order to be confident in what we do. We need to be willing to accept that other people are still learning too. We need to be understanding of others and of ourselves. When we are having trouble redirecting anxiety, stress, or letting go of a situation and we are not sure how to overcome it, we can ask ourselves, "Did I try my best?" Sometimes that is all we can do and that should be enough. If the answer is "yes," we can take comfort in the fact that we put our best foot forward. We need to accept reassurance from ourselves that we made our decision and it was the best we could make at that time. Wait... How about if the answer is "no?" Then, we need to ask ourselves, "what could I have done to improve the outcome?" This answer will allow us to be better prepared in the future, if we encounter the problem or situation again. But, don't dwell on the "could've" and "should've" because we have learned what to do moving forward. Now, it's time to forgive ourselves and progress onward. One thing to be careful about is displaying to much false confidence because this can resemble arrogance. In the event that we recognize that we might be coming across a bit arrogant, we need to make an effort to correct it. We don't want to let the guilt seep in and prevent us from gaining the self-confidence we need to lift ourselves up. We all try not to loose emotional control. But, the important thing to do, if we do, is to redirect ourselves and move forward. The key factor in self-confidence is simple. Do NOT let self-doubt keep us from taking a step forward. It takes time to embrace new habits, therefore, we need to embrace our set-backs as part of our progress moving forward.

Chapter Two

THE

INNER

WARMTH

Love thyself!

Each individual has their own unique interpretation of the meaning of love. Sometimes it can be difficult to capture the true essence of an emotion by attempting to define or quantify it. Most people can probably agree that love represents a strong emotional affection and a benevolent state of virtue from the simplest deed to an awe-inspiring fulfillment. we generally take the time to convey our love towards the one's we hold dear (parents, spouse, family, friends, pets, etc.,) through small acts of kindness everyday. We let them know that they're worthy and deserving of our love. We want them to know that we appreciate them and that provides us with a sense of fulfillment. It's important that we treat ourselves with that same kindness and affection. It's also important that we become content with our own independent mind set. Once we are conscious of our own feelings and desires, we are able to accept ourselves and others on a deeper level. We begin to understand that happiness truly begins within. It's the relationship we create with our selves that will ultimately bring contentment and satisfy our yearning for happiness. How does this improve our external relationships? Once we accept ourselves; we accept ourselves wholeheartedly, complete with our faults and our flaws. This allows us to release our own emotional insecurities and form more intimate relationships. Once we're able to accept our own insecurities and relinquish our own defenses, we can welcome love more genuinely. We can develop a deeper, intimate relationship with ourselves and with others. Love has a way of transforming our existence. To truly develop a healthy relationship we need to include ourselves in our relationship. We need to stop feeling guilty for loving ourselves. There is a difference between selfless or unconditional love and self-sacrifice. Sacrificing our own passions and aspirations repeatedly in the name of love is not healthy. We hear people say things, such as: God wants them to sacrifice all the things that they desire and put themselves last. These people feel an obligation to set aside their own aspirations in the fulfillment of others. A need to constantly put other people's needs above their own. In some manner this action is conceived as devotion. In many situations a selfless act is considered a good thing. However, we must remember to consider our own well-being, and not overlook and neglect ourselves in the process of helping others. At times, we may have a tendency to over look ourselves and we're not realizing that we're creating an injustice to ourselves. When we constantly put ourselves last, other people subconsciously put us last. People become accustom to us allowing their preferences to precede that of our own. Therefore, they may begin to automatically appropriate that manner of thinking and fail to consider our feelings. It may become a natural disposition for others to fail to conceive our thoughts, feelings, or concerns

surrounding a situation or circumstance. At this point,

we're no longer consciously contributing to the act of

selfishness. Instead, we're being over-looked and

neglected. We deserve to be noticed and considered by

those around us. In the event that we find ourselves

being taken for granted, we need to make sure that we

express our feelings to those around us in a positive

manner. We need to let others know that we want an

opportunity to contribute to a situation or event. Most

of the time people are not consciously dismissing us.

They have simply become accustom to our own

behavioral patterns. Therefore, if we constantly choose

to put other people's needs and wants before our own,

other people will often do the same. Once we start recognizing that this is occurring, we need to make a conscious effort to correct it. How? By becoming self-aware and paying attention to our own needs, as well as the needs of others, we can ensure that we receive the self-love and care that we deserve. Being able to love and appreciate ourselves ensures that we are not willingly contributing to self-neglect emotionally or other wise. God's greatest commandment tells us to love our neighbor in the same manner that we would love ourselves. There is no confusion in what God is telling us to do. He wants us to love ourselves. He doesn't want us to neglect ourselves. He doesn't say neglect your neighbor as you would neglect yourself. It is important not to over- extenuate ourselves when doing for others. It's great to want to help others but it isn't great if we are hurting ourselves in the process. It is important that we make a conscious effort to love and respect ourselves. The idea of depriving ourselves gifts, vacations, celebrations, etc., because it may come across as selfish is preposterous. We should celebrate ourselves. God gave us life and it is something to celebrate. Life can definitely be overwhelming at times. We can get caught up in all the hustle and bustle of daily routines. Therefore, it's important to take time for ourselves and relax. We need to set aside time to rest our physical and spiritual selves. There are many different ways people find time to relax. Some people

31

set aside quiet time to pray every morning. Some people set aside time to meditate every morning. Some people just set aside time in the morning to quietly process their thoughts and drink their coffee. The time we allocate to our self each day can help us mentally prepare for any obstacles that we encounter during the day. It can help us counteract stress, stay positive, and enhance our overall well-being. There is no shame in requiring time for our own well-being. It's true that we can be our own worse enemy at times. Our own self approach can make it difficult for us to take the time we need for ourselves. Especially, if we don't make a habit of setting aside time for ourselves. Have you ever thought, "I am going to lay in bed all day or read a book?" Perhaps, you want to sit and relax in your favorite chair and watch television. Have you noticed that negative thoughts start to creep into your mind? Our internal critic will start to nag... (nag...nag...nag...) More than likely reminding us about all of our unfinished chores. Nagging about those dirty dishes that are sitting in the sink, or the lawn that needs mowing. Our own inner voice will start to remind us of all the things that we could be doing instead of relaxing. The truth is… Those dishes aren't going anywhere and the lawn can be mowed another day. We don't have to ignore the chores forever to take some much needed time to relax. However, we do need to remain mindful of our interior critic because it's always going to try and keep us from relaxing. Our health and well-being is extremely important. We often hear people refer to procrastination as an inferior quality. We witness people praising others for being proactive, driven, and energetic. This outlook causes some people to confuse relaxation for procrastination. It's great to motivate people to get their task done quickly. However, our health and well-being is one of the most urgent task of all. We shouldn't be so eager to put off our own well being. Our perception of importance can prioritize our responses towards our goals. The way we look at things can change our understanding of them. For example: Most parents have a habit of tending to their child's needs before they tend to their own needs. The thought of doing otherwise can be appalling. However, in the event that a parent has to take a flight to another state with their child, a flight attendant will go over the safety procedure of the airline. During the instructions, the flight attendant may advise all the parents on the plane to put their oxygen mask on first before helping their child put on their mask. This advice will come as a shock to a lot of parents because their perception depicts that the child's needs should come first. However, once the attendant explains that if the parent passes out before getting the oxygen mask on the child, both of them will die. This will open a new insight on how a parent will view the situation. Parents know that there is a level of self-sacrificing required with raising children. Parents have to put aside a lot of their own wants and desires to ensure their children live a happy and healthy life. But, it is important to remember that parents also have to tend to themselves first to ensure they remain capable of tending to the needs of their children. It is important that we take time for ourselves and maintain our own well-being. The good thing is that it is never to late to start loving ourselves. Self-love was once perceived as vain. Whereas, it's widely understood today that self-love is important to maintain a healthy and balanced life. People who practice self-love tend to be more happy and more resilient. Some people feel undeserving of love due to lack of success in a career or a romance. That is when it is really important to remember that no job can define us and not everyone is going to understand us. We can't take on other peoples expectations of us and we shouldn't be comparing ourselves to others. We should aspire to improve ourselves to become a better person today than we were yesterday. We should strive to build a positive self-concept of our self. The best way we can stay committed to ourselves is to ensure that we don't allow other people's perception of us to define us. Keep in mind that some people will hold onto our past mistakes and attempt to remind us of those mistakes over and over. When we dwell on past mistakes it can hinder us from moving forward. The fact that other people cannot move beyond the past, doesn't mean that we can't... News flash... It's in the past! We grow, our bodies grow, our intelligence grows, our mentality grows, our emotional intelligence grows, and our wisdom grows. Some people will try to dampen our growth by reminding us of something that we may have done as a young child or teenager. That type of thinking reveals a limited mentality. The past is olden and the future is golden. Therefore, we need to learn to put the past behind us. Do you know how many people would be suffering with despair, if they held onto every mistake they have ever made? (Especially, during childhood). Of course, the question is rhetorical. Yesterday was in the past, tomorrow is the future and today we are trying to figure it out. We should all try to take a few moments every day to consider, 'what does' and 'doesn't' make us feel good about ourselves. Therefore, we can focus on the positive things that make us feel good and remain constantly aware of what direction that we want to center our attention on. We can focus on forgiving ourselves often, loving ourselves daily, and continuing to move forward. There are many small actions that can be implemented in a daily routine that allows us to focus on ourselves. One of the most important steps is to realize the importance of embracing self-love. Knowing you are worthy of celebration. Being able to accept gifts is also an important factor in self-love. It's easy to decline a gift someone is offering us.

Especially, if we don't feel worthy. Now, if the gift is too extravagant, nicely declining could be interpreted as social graces. But, some people feel really uncomfortable accepting gifts or allowing someone to treat them to a meal. It's okay to accept it and appreciate it. Unless you feel there are unwanted attachments included. The social norm would be to say, "Thank you!" It provides the giver a chance to be helpful or share their love with the gift of giving. There is no need to feel guilty about accepting something for ourselves. It is important to be both a gracious giver and receiver of gifts. When we give something to someone, we receive a gift in return, the gift of joy (it can make us feel good about being able to make

someone else happy). Therefore, it's a good thing to

accept a gift so someone else can also experience the

joy that comes from giving. It isn't the object that is

the real gift, but the fact that it was for us.

Chapter Three

RECOGNIZE

THE

CHAMPION

WITHIN

Accept thyself!

Once we start to realize, understand, and accept that we do have talent and potential, we are on the threshold of uncovering our ideal selves. Everyone is different. Everyone has different talents in different areas. Self-actualization is a concept of understanding ones self. Some people have a natural gift for counting numbers. Some people have a natural gift for drawing. Some people can tell great stories. When we begin to recognize our own talents, we are opening the door to our passions. When we begin to recognize our own passions, we are opening the doorway to our purpose.

A programmer needs to program, a builder needs to build, a writer needs to write, if they're to feel fulfilled. We need to follow our passion within in order to satisfy our internal yearning. When we purposely follow our dreams we're developing our own gratification. When we feel discontent with what we are doing it's more than likely because it isn't our purpose. Think about it on a physical platform of anatomy. Some people are born with denser bones and muscles. They can move a boulder easier than someone that is smaller boned with a moderate muscle build. That doesn't mean someone with a smaller build couldn't dedicate themselves to muscle strengthening and eventually move the boulder. It just means some things come easier to some, than to others. Our genetics and our surroundings influence our abilities. Different people thrive in different circumstances. A fish needs water to live. When we take a fish out of water, it will die. Take a monkey from a tree and throw it into the ocean, it will probably drown. The same thing goes in regards to comparing ourselves to others. Each person has his/her own talents. A monkey that worries because it cannot swim like a fish will always feel disappointed in itself. A fish that mopes because it can not walk on land will always be displeased with itself. Of course, humans are neither fish nor monkeys, but we're all different. A tall man can reach a high book-shelf with no assistance. A short man may need a stool. The trouble with comparing ourselves to others is that it may lead to self-disappointment. It can lead us to feeling inadequate. There is always going to be someone better than us. And, there is always going to be someone that cannot do something as well as us. It is best to progress by comparing ourselves to our past selves. We should always continue to work on our selves and encourage others to do the same. We need to try to make a habit of nurturing and understanding ourselves. It helps to improve our own self-awareness and allows us to become familiar with ourselves.

FOCUS ON POSITIVE AFFIRMATIONS & AVOID

NEGATIVE SELF TALK

POSITIVE <==========> **NEGATIVE**

CAN DO <==========> **CAN'T DO**

CONFIDENCE <==========> **FEAR**

PASSION <==========> **APATHY**

ACCEPTANCE <==========> **DENIAL**

FORGIVE <==========> **BLAME**

GROWTH <==========> **RESISTANCE**

DIGNITY <=========> **SHAME**

KEY: POSITIVE SELF REFLECTION & VISUALIZATION

To efficiently become aware of our own strengths and weaknesses, we need to self-analyze and focus on our own abilities. Remember, this isn't about being the smartest, fastest, or strongest. It is about self growth and our own metamorphosis. Therefore we would want to take note of all our good qualities. We could start by asking ourselves, "How forgiving am I?" This can provide us with a starting point on self-forgiveness. The likelihood of us letting go of the past mistakes that we've made and forgiving ourselves for the future mistakes we're sure to make. We will make mistakes. Therefore, we can acclaim our efforts and forgive our mistakes. There is no limit on achieving personal growth. It is a never ending constant progression. The way we view ourselves and the way we treat ourselves

is learned behavior. We can change the way we

behave. It's important that we accept ourselves, but

that doesn't mean to stop improving ourselves.

Personal growth improves self awareness and it helps

us to identify the person that we yearn to become. It's

always a great idea to make a commitment to our own

personal growth. We can establish a plan that is fun

and exhilarating. There are going to be times that we

will not feel like staying committed to change or

focusing on learning new things. We are naturally

resistant to change. Taking small steps and celebrating

our achievements is a way to keep us involved in our

commitment and it also prevents us from becoming

discouraged. The expectation of over night achievements and fast transformation can divert our objectives. Which can lead to frustration and disappointment. Set backs are normal, if we feel we are slipping into old habits, we need to recognize it and redirect ourselves. We can redirect ourselves back on track to our self improvement goals. The truly important thing is to not give up. Personal growth is not a short term plan. It is a continuous path of development. We generally fear change and resist it because it can be terrifying sometimes. We may need to convince ourselves to step forward and step out of our comfort zone. It's okay for us to lean on friends and family members to help keep us motivated. The encouragement that we receive from the people we love can take us a long way in achieving our personal goals. However, remember the most important thing is that we're happy with the changes we're making, and we're taking the time to appreciate ourselves along the way. We need to always take the time to celebrate ourselves daily. Ensure that we appreciate every milestone and set back in our journey. For example... I see a pair of pants that I absolutely love. I say to myself, "when I loose twenty pounds I will buy those pants." However, I may never loose twenty pounds and I may never get those pants. But, if I buy those pants to fit me now. I will absolutely still love those pants. And, if I still love those pants after I loose twenty pounds, I can always buy another pair that will fit me just right. I'll have the pleasure of wearing the style all over again. We need to celebrate ourselves for who we are today and who we will be tomorrow.

Chapter Four

THE FORTUNATE

CIRCUMSTANCES

TO

UNFORTUNATE

EVENTS

Gratitude!

Being able to deliberately cultivate the idea of living a grateful life can actually increase our overall well-being. A lot of emphasis has been placed on gratitude and how it relates to the improvement of one's mental and physical well-being. People that practice gratitude tend to be more happier and live a more resilient life. But, it's our priorities in life that ultimately determine the intensity of our happiness, as we practice gratitude. People who are grateful for the simple necessities in life, such as: shelter, food, water, and health tend to live happier lives. People who share the belief that life, itself, is a blessing also tend to enjoy life a little more than those that take life for granted. Have you ever noticed that they tend to carry a higher level of optimism and have a tendency to practice gratitude unconsciously? Usually, it's because of the way in which they have been taught to appreciate the simple things in life and the idea that life, itself, is precious. Therefore, the way in which they perceive life promotes the concept that anything above and beyond the necessities of life is an extra blessing. Most of them are taught to value the fundamental basic essentials at an early age in life and are redirected to appreciate the significance of the things that are vital to their survival. Some, if not all, are reared to recognize that human life is a gift and should be treasured above all else.

Therefore, they're able to find a higher level of joy and

appreciation in their own existence and the existence

of others. Ergo, their success and purpose in life isn't

defined by materialistic objects, expensive jewelry,

and/or the need to feel more important than their

fellow counterpart. When their basic needs are meet

and they're surrounded by the people they love, they

feel like the happiest people in the world. This notion

encourages a certain degree of wonderment and

blissfulness that cultivates an optimistic view of the

future. It's for that reason that the people who are

influenced by these particular beliefs can experience

almost the exact same disappointment and/or hardship

that someone who doesn't share in this belief may experience, and still appear to remain more enthusiastic and hopeful toward their future. The people who share in this belief experience the same feelings of disappointment, discouragement, despair, sadness, sense of burden, and other feelings of inadequacies that a person that doesn't share in this belief would experience. But, they have been taught to focus on the things in life that make them happy and not the things that make them sad. They have been trained to become aware of counterproductive feelings and to redirect those feelings toward something constructive in their life that they can control and not to focus on the things they have no control over. They take comfort in the thought that they're still alive. And, most of them are religious and have faith in a higher power. They have faith in the Lord and they maintain trust that the Lord will provide even when things appear disheartening. It can be difficult to discern when they're struggling because they're capable of drawing an inner strength from their faith in connection with their appreciation of life, itself. In return it provides them with a certain feeling of security and acceptance that some people spend a great portion of their lives yearning for. The fact that they value people over objects amplifies their contentment. They already have an understanding that our general appreciation level is amplified when we're surrounded by the people in our life that we love (family and friends). The mutual emotional bond and support that we share with one another has a way of intensifying our joy. Living a grateful life is the key to a happy life and there are many reasons to be thankful. Of course, our level of gratitude does extend as our wishes are fulfilled, such as: receiving chocolate, getting a new bike, owning a car, having a house, or traveling on vacation. Usually, our level of happiness rises as our appreciation expands and we recognize new reasons to be grateful. It maybe that we are grateful for the strong community of neighbors or fellow church members. It could be something as random as the weather. Maybe a farmer appreciates the rain because his crops need the rain to grow. Maybe Sarah decided to get married on the beach and the day turned out beautiful. Maybe the day wasn't beautiful like the forecast predicted and it started raining. Everyone had to squeeze in under the canopy. To Sarah's surprise it brought everyone closer; everyone laughed, joked, huddled together, and began telling stories from the past. It turned out better than she could have ever imagined. Things do not always have to work out as planned in order to still be great. We can appreciate a lot more, if we take the time to look at it from a different perspective. Our perspective on life determines our outlook most of the time. The practice of being grateful provides an optimistic, hopeful, and pleasant outlook. It does have impact on an individual's happiness. What is gratitude and how do we practice it? It is the willingness to appreciate and reciprocate kindness. Therefore, we could start by simply practicing our manners and being polite. Generally, as children, we are taught the fundamentals of social decorum: saying please, thank you, you're welcome, excuse me, bless you, offering a helping hand, and other like wise etiquette. We just have to remember to make use of them. In America, we celebrate Thanksgiving every year to observe a festival held by the Pilgrims. Normally, we take the time to consider the things that we're grateful for and gather around those that we love to show our appreciation. Therefore, the concept of gratitude is relatively understood. It's simply a matter of being thankful and being kind. This outlook is known to promote an optimistic view of life and ultimately a happier life. We can have two different individuals, we can open a box of cookies, and offer each individual a cookie. One individual will be grateful that we decided to share a cookie with them. However, we may find that the other individual is disappointed and hurt because we only gave them one cookie. The first individual practicing gratitude understood that until we gave them a cookie they had none at all. Therefore, they perceived our action as thoughtful and considerate. While, the second individual seeing us with an entire pack of cookies perceived us as greedy, even though, we shared a cookie with them. The first individual is more than likely going to speak respectfully to others on our behalf. Whereas, the second individual will more than likely spread unwanted rumors related to our greed and selfishness. Unfortunately, this can cause discord among many people that wasn't even present at the time we shared the cookies. The first individual probably assumed that we intended to share the cookies with other people. It made them feel content with the notion that other individuals will also taste the delicious sweetness. The second person apparently assumed the worse and felt righteous in revealing our greed. We can take the to time to explain to the second individual that more people are coming and we plan to share a cookie with them. This may prevent them from assuming the worse. However, it is easy to perceive that the individual that practices gratitude is happier than the individual who may struggle with the concept. We're all guilty of forgetting to appreciate the small things in our lives at times. It's important that we keep trying to maintain a grateful mindset. It provides a harmonious outlook and a joyful state of mind. These teachings have been around for a really long time. Most of the religions have been emphasizing on gratitude and other virtues throughout history. A scientific study becoming popular, called positive psychology, places an emphasis on gratitude and other virtues. It acknowledges the connection of being grateful and living happy. Thus, science is exploring the spiritual and emotional aspects of the human life, expanding the acceptance of human emotions and the need for virtues. The exploration science is taking into the metaphysical realm of reasoning disproves the century-old rumor that science and religion clash with one another. The spiritual and the mundane are interconnected. There are many different approaches regarding gratitude that can be found from various sources: religious, ethics, philosophy, science and more. In which there is a mutual understanding that gratitude is an extremely beneficial asset in our daily lives. The bible instructs us to give thanks daily and rejoice in each day. Ancient philosophers also suggest

65

that gratitude is the foundation to a virtuous life. Therefore, we do know that the practice of gratitude goes back over two millenniums. And, it's still being promoted today. Those that attempt to argue that the precept on gratitude is merely a sectarian craze are indeed disoriented with the fact that this concept is clearly not a short-lived novice phase. On the contrary, it's a natural characteristic of our being and should be embraced. How do we embrace gratitude? We take time each day to think about and rejoice in the people and things in our life that make us happy. Then, we take time to consider a manner for which we can express our appreciation through kind words and/or actions. This will encourage us to consistently direct our thoughts towards the people and things in our lives that make us feel fortunate and prevent us from surrendering to negative emotions as we're faced with adversities. These memories induce a certain level of nostalgia that stimulates a reassuring view of the future. How do we learn more about gratitude? There are many ways to develop our understanding: reading books, researching in a library or online, taking classes, gaining experiences, having discussions, going to church, and more. Thankfully with the modern technology of our century, we have readily accessible information through the internet. The popularity of the internet has expanded the world wide web to almost every location throughout the world. The information is vast and all we have to do is look for it. This makes it easier to acquire knowledge for continuous growth and personal development. There are many courses online providing a social setting in which users can interact with other users. These courses can be a great experience for everyone. Especially, those seeking to explore guidance and camaraderie along their route to personal growth and development. Being that we're social creatures by nature, it maybe beneficial to interconnect with other people. The information is usually accessible according to the individuals preference and association. A person interested in learning more about God can explore gratitude and other virtues through the practice of religions, which can be found online and/or in person at a church, temple or chapel in their community. An individual interested in the scientific clarification or a philosophers explication can also use the internet to further their understanding and probably find courses available at their local colleges. There are many methods to obtain the information but it's ultimately up to us to embrace it and make use of it. Practicing gratitude requires a progressive mindset, therefore, we need to take the time to actively think about and appreciate the things in our lives that make us happy.

Chapter Five

LOOK TO

THY SELF

FOR

REVELATION

Know thyself!

Are we philosophers of our own lives? After all, we devote a lot of our time and attention to understanding our own reality and existence. Each person is essential to their own thoughts and perception. Socrates was an ancient philosopher. He was a moral philosopher that stressed the importance of examining and reflecting on life, as we experience it. Each and every single person has probably derived some sort of philosophy in regards to their own goals in life. Most people have probably designed those goals around their own conception of happiness. Because, most people simply want to do good and be happy. But, in order to really examine our own lives, we need to look deep within ourselves for the answer. Understanding ourselves on a deeper level entails knowing where we stand in life. Being aware of our values, our likes and dislikes are all part of understanding ourselves. Our values determine our character; our likes and dislikes determine our happiness. How can we be happy, if we don't know what makes us happy? To truly understand ourselves we have to inspect ourselves. What does that mean? It's almost impossible for us to find anything if we're unsure about what we're looking for in the first place. How do we know something is missing, unless we look to ensure it's there? Some people probably believe that this sounds absolutely absurd. How does someone not know what they like or don't like? Unfortunately, Many people find themselves disengaged from their internal selves in one way or another. Some people tend to get absorbed in pleasing other people and often forget about themselves. This happens more than we would like to believe. Therefore, it's important to take time everyday to observe exactly what is currently going on in our lives and exactly how we feel about our life in it's present state. This routine will allow us to be present in the moment. It will aid us in remaining mindfully aware of our feelings surrounding the ongoing conditions of our lives. It enables us to deliberate on the reasons we think and feel a certain way. How will this help?

Helen was a young wife and mother. She was devoted to her family and she considered herself happy. She placed a lot of emphasis on ensuring that her family was happy. She became enthralled with fulfilling their needs and desires. And, as time progressed she became extremely accommodating. This is a character trait found in some of the most loved mothers throughout the world. However, her willingness to accommodate on such great levels induced a certain lack of interest or detachment in regards to her own interest. Over time she became dispassionate with herself, and she couldn't decide on what she liked or didn't like. She knew exactly what everyone else liked and disliked.

Her family loved her and they would urge her to buy something for herself, or they would ask her what she wanted. But, her answer was always vague and usually concluded with something that everyone could enjoy. It wasn't until her family persisted that she select a gift that was meant only for herself, one that she would like and enjoy, that she realize she had become unacquainted with herself. As she walked through the store, she noticed she would get overly enthusiastic when she come across things another person would enjoy. But, in that moment she also realized that she had no idea what she wanted. Obviously, she found eagerness in making other people happy. Nonetheless, it was evident that she was unfamiliar with her own likes and dislikes. She couldn't discern a suitable gift for herself. It was an enlightening moment in her life. An alarming feeling came over her, as she realized, she had become a stranger to herself. How is it possible for someone to become impassive with themselves? Truthfully, it's not very hard. Sometimes we extend our selves too much in order to please other people that we forget to please our selves. We often overlook the importance of the small things that we enjoy and the fact that they have any relevance at all. Therefore, overtime we become accustom to relinquishing our own small pleasures to indulge others, as the sentiment appears insignificant. Ordinarily the small things seem inconsequential. Thus, we decide to avoid conflict and be agreeable. But, to what extent? Helen may prefer mayonnaise and someone else may prefer salad dressing. The other person maybe overly adamant about their opinion that salad dressing is the best and blatantly refuses to use mayonnaise. Although, Helen would prefer the mayonnaise she is extremely complaisant and chooses the salad dressing. In doing so she avoids discord and maintains an amicable relationship. Therefore, does it really matter? Not, if it's every once in a while. Nevertheless, if it becomes a pattern, it generally will develop into a habit. The reason Helen expressed a tendency to suppress the things she liked in order to oblige other people was because overtime she stifled her own desires until it became difficult for her to make a decision in favor of herself. It eventually resulted in an inability to make beneficial choices in connection with herself, her passions, and her dreams. It all began to appear inconsequential. She became indecisive and reluctant to fulfill her own desires. Mostly because she was unaware and indifferent to fulfilling them. Recognizing this she unleashed her emotions and became a bit emotional. She rationalized the irrational. To understand her feelings she had to allow them to surface and analyze them. She began to take the time she needed to think about what she was feeling and examine why she was feeling this particular way. This helped her to evaluate her feelings and her responses to determine what she favored and disfavored. She learned to always include herself when she made a decision and to be aware of her preferences when making them. In order to maintain a good understanding of ourselves we need to take the time to consider our own thoughts, feelings, and motives. We can try taking time to explore what we're thinking about through out our day and try to determine why we're thinking about it. How do we view it and why do we view it that way? After we take a moment to examine our own perspective, we can ask ourselves, do we like our perspective? Would it be a perspective that we would want to promote? Is there any thing particular that we would want to change? It may sound

79

quite foolish. However, when we close our mind off to the understanding and accepting of alternative possibilities we're limiting ourselves. Many of us at one time or another have formulated an opinion about someone only to find out later that our opinion was incorrect. Our perceptions can limit us, if we're unwilling to open our minds to the truth and overcome our conception of the truth. We tend to justify our actions and decisions around our own personal beliefs and we have a tendency to self-justify our stance. This is why it's important that we understand ourselves. To know what we hold high opinions on, or what we truly believe. Because, if we make a decision that is against our inner beliefs, it can cause inner tension. We can have an unstable reaction that will cause us to over react. Inner conflict occurs if we're not in agreement with our internal selves. Self-justification does help us to develop and maintain a balanced self-concept most of the time. In the event that we're not able to justify our actions to our internal selves, we cause a dissatisfaction of our selves. Thus, prompting insecurities that spawn negative emotions such as resentment, envy, and jealousy. Subsequently, we develop a tendency to judge others more harshly. We want to feel that they're breaking our morale code more than we're violating it, ourselves. We find ourselves desperately seeking a certain level of personal vindication because we have violated our own moral principles. We have a profound desire to justify

our wrongdoing. We want to ease and alleviate the

feelings of guilt emerging from within ourselves. The

guilt caused by our own transgressions against our

selves. Therefore, it's not just a desire to pacify our

internal guilt but a need to feel righteous. But, judging

others is not going to clear a guilty conscience. Nor,

will it absolve our guilt. As long as we continue to

search outside of ourselves for a desirable solution by

blaming others and reflecting hatred, it will only

continue to perpetuate an undesirable outcome. A

restless heart cannot be content. We need to go easy on

ourselves and surrender the internal turmoil. How? By

practicing forgiveness, acceptance, and appreciation.

We can also prevent internal conflict by understanding our own moral philosophy on life, and making decisions that coincide with our own personal standards. Remaining mindful of our own thoughts and feelings prior to making a decision enables us the opportunity to ensure that our decision will not conflict with our own moral existence.

VIRTUES

LOVE

INSPIRATION

FORGIVENESS

JOY

LOYALTY

HOPE

COURAGE

KINDNESS

COMPASSION

GRACE

RESPECT

AWE

Traits that define moral principles.

Life is all about making decisions and sometime our choices may not produce the outcome we're intending. But, that is okay. We simply make the best choice that we can at the time and we try to ensure that our choice aligns with our values. And, if we find ourselves having to make a difficult decision, we can ask someone close to us for advice. Someone we know may have encountered a similar situation and maybe able to understand our position. We're social creatures and we need each other to grow. One man alone did not cultivate civilization, it took many. Therefore, if we have someone to turn to for comfort and support, we should value their opinion. Everyone feels a little self conscious at times; it's during those times, we could really benefit from the support of those around us. We all go through difficult situations at one time or another. We don't always feel confident in making a decision. Some actually find it easier to avoid a difficult situation. But, it's better to make a decision to do something rather than do nothing at all. Some may feel they're putting themselves in a vulnerable position by disclosing their personal concerns with another person. This is an honest feeling. We need to feel comfortable in confiding in someone. We want to feel confident that we can trust them because it provides us a sense of security with sharing private details of our lives. Therefore, if we don't have someone with whom we feel comfortable confiding in, we can find self-motivators to keep us feeling happy, busy, and accomplished. This can help us ignite the courage we need to make a decision. Because tasking ourselves with a goal ensures that we will have to make many small decisions in completing that goal. Thus, building our decision-making skills and enabling ourselves to become more decisive. It can be something as simple as getting around to a chore we've been dreading to do, a hobby, or a small project that we've been putting off. Our internal voice that loves to hound us will eventually boost our motivation. We can rely on our internal critic to be useful for many things, as long as it's not filling our thoughts with self-doubt. But, we get to choose which thoughts we want to focus on and which ones we want to ignore. Our ability to make choices is one of the best things ever. *FREEWILL!* We have to be able to think for our selves and learn to make good choices. There are a lot of adults who find decision making difficult. Some people have trouble making a decision and some people obsess over the decision they've made. Did they make the right one? They worry that it will not work out. Some will constantly second guess their decision. Everyone makes decisions daily. Let's think back on what we have covered... People make mistakes. It's okay if it doesn't work out. Have faith that it will work out. If it doesn't, have faith that there is a better solution that we haven't thought of and don't give up... The freedom to make our own choices determine and guide our lives. If we feel more comfortable asking for advice from people around us, then we can ask for advice. However, the ultimate choice over our own life is ours. And, we need to keep ourselves in mind when making a decision. Some people hesitate when making a decision based on a historical pattern of bad decisions. They fear the consequences of making the decision. This is where self-confidence comes in and personal growth. The past is the past. We recognize, forgive, and move forward. The ability to truly live our own lives is based on our ability to make our own choices. One of the best ways to make good choices for ourselves is to be self-aware. What makes me happy?

Imagine how our own decision will affect our own well-being. The significance of thinking positively will also impact the outcome. We can override our own internal critic by using hope and faith. Our subconscious influences our decision and the outcome of the choices that we make. We want to encompass ourselves with good vibrations. Why is it hard for some people to feel positive? Why do some people appear to emit negativity? People express symptoms of negative emotions because of extensive internal guilt. There's a specific region of the brain that is influential in regulating these emotions. People with a higher degree of sensitivity towards other peoples feelings and emotions tend to have a higher level of activity in this region of the brain. An increase of activity in this region can prevent someone from communicating properly. This can cause them to concentrate more on the chances of a negative outcome based on their decision which negates the value of a possible positive outcome. It's easy to view them as negative because of their constant expectations of a pessimistic outcome. People struggling with this internal conflict may express an inclination to criticize themselves, display feelings of helplessness, or begin projecting their own negative emotions onto others. This is not a permanent state of emotional reality. People prone to this behavior can overcome the negative emotional essence of this condition. How? Learned behavior and habits is one of the best ways to overcome these feelings. Being self-aware of one's own negative emotional state provides an opportunity to transform negative emotions into positive emotions. Again, we're social creatures by nature and having other people around us who's willing to love or care for us does makes a huge difference. We need to stay open to their feedback because it can assist us in recognizing when negative emotions are surfacing. The reassurance and understanding that we receive can go a long way in helping us refocus our energy. But, the ability to change always comes from within ourselves. Because, we're the true philosophers of our own lives and we're responsible for the way we think.

Chapter Six

LET

THE

SUN

SHINE

Smile!

Smiling and laughing is essentially the easiest way that we can enhance our overall health. Smiling is directly linked to maintaining an optimistic and positive outlook on life. It can calm our nervous system and negate stress related anxieties. Did you know that when we laugh and smile that our brains actually release neurotransmitters such as: dopamine, endorphins, and serotonin? Yes, a simple laugh or smile will generate the release of these chemicals in our body. These chemicals are known to reduce our blood pressure, heart rate and calm our nervous system. The affirmation that laughter is the best medicine has been evinced in the use of science. It can increase both our physical and mental health. The diverse benefits of a simple laugh or smile are vast, such things as: boosting the immunity, easing anxiety, strengthening resilience, lowering stress, improving moods, and much more. But what if we don't have any reason to smile or laugh? The best thing is that it doesn't have to be an involuntary response or unexpected laugh. Even a fake voluntary laugh response can increase oxygen to our brains. Therefore, we can consider smiling and laughing to be a form of exercise, an activity in which we do to improve our overall health and fitness. Think of different ways that a person can increase the amount of times that they smile or laugh in a single day. It can be such things as:

watching television comedies, going out to a comedy club, hanging out with friends that love to laugh, sharing jokes with loved ones, laughing at the silly things we do, or simply setting aside time to exercise a laugh. After making a list, try to practice one or two ideas a day to personally assess the theory. Many cities actually have a laughter yoga course which promotes laughter as a form of physical exercise. And, it's common knowledge that exercise is considered a key factor to a healthy life. But who knew that exercise could consist of something as easy as a smile or laugh? This surely eliminates a lot of excuses to exercise. Another tactic used by many people to intensify their own joy is to simply participate in boosting the happiness of the people around them. By finding ways to participate in the encouragement and happiness of other people it simultaneously provides them with a certain feeling of meaningfulness which creates positive emotions within themselves. Researchers have confirmed that there's a connection between being kind to others and a higher degree of happiness within oneself. It genuinely enhances one's own overall well-being. When we do something good for someone else or we take part in someone's happiness it triggers a reward stimuli within ourselves. The receptors within the nucleus accumbens of our brains release dopamine. The chemical, dopamine, plays a vital part in our overall well-being. What are ways to proactively demonstrate kindness? Become customary to providing sincere compliments to others. It can be in person, electronically, or in writing. It is important that the compliments are sincere this ensures an authentic emotional link that promotes a rewarding stimuli. How do we provide an authentic compliment? We look for the good in others. When we make a cognitive decision to look for the good in someone, we normally will find an attribute to praise. Another reason it is necessary to ensure that we're providing genuine compliments is because some people are not open and receptive to compliments. People with low self-esteem issues that have a negative self-image probably already feel uncomfortable with being presented with a compliment. Therefore, if the compliment comes across as insincere it may have a reverse emotional impact from what we initially intended. Instead of it being perceived as a polite gesture, it may come across as an emotional manipulation tactic. This could bring about an unfavorable view and skepticism towards our motive in complimenting them. Therefore, it is extremely important that the compliment is genuine. The benefits of an authentic compliment allows the receiver to view us as trustworthy. Providing an insincere compliment to a person, known to have a high level of self-esteem, will also promote mistrust. Unless, someone has a specific reason to be regarded as a person who uses fictitious praise to fulfill their own self-interest, it is best that the compliments be authentic. A good compliment goes deeper than the first thing you notice about a person. Take a moment to really notice what you truly admire about the person. Please make the compliment genuine and deliver it with sincerity. Try to make a cognitive point to stay away from passive-aggressive compliments. It is extremely easy to hurt someone's feelings without even realizing it. Therefore, try to be mindful on how the compliment is being perceived. For example: Sally came to work today wearing a new pair of red heals. Helen attempting to compliment Sally said, "I really like your new shoes. But, what made you pick red?" This rather signifies that Helen didn't actually like the red shoes much at all. The compliment caused an adverse impact. Sally got really defensive in her response in defending her red shoes. A lot of people probably wouldn't think much about prompting a simple question to open up dialog in an attempt to build rapport. Unfortunately, verbal expression can often lead to misunderstandings. This can cause barriers in building relationships. However, being aware that people are often trying to connect with us and understanding that their intentions are good does allow us to respond without offense. Sometimes it's the manner in which we express ourselves verbally that leads to a misunderstanding and sometimes it's the perception of the percipient themselves that results in a misinterpretation. However, when we take time to accept others, we take less offense in regards to their responses. Thus, prompting good conversation and developing a connection. Keep in mind that kindness can come in many forms via words and actions. There are many simple actions that can go a long way towards boosting someone's day such as: holding a door open, a smile, or a nod. These small gestures express a positive vibe that can be felt and shared by other people. And, it does contribute to our overall well being. Believe it or not, so does bragging. But, wait... Isn't that statement a contradiction to the social norms of our society? Why? A stereotypical view of narcissism has been associated with bragging. Only people with low moral standard boast. No one wants to appear to be a glory seeker. Who dictated that it's okay to boast our imperfections, but not our achievements? How does this successfully influence us to grow mentally and emotionally? Everyone should be able to express pride and happiness in themselves. Everyone should feel good about acclaiming and proclaiming their achievements. If we feel proud of our performance, accomplishments, victory, etc., Then, we should announce it with passion. Just remain tactfully aware of how our self-pride maybe perceived by those around us. It's a wonderful thing to sincerely boast and share our achievement, but, gloating isn't acceptable. People have a tendency to mistake self-praise for gloating. There's a difference in the intention and the nature between the two. The people that really love us are eager to see us achieve. The naysayers... Well... They are naysayers. So... we should be grateful when our mom, spouse, brother, sister, son, daughter, uncle, cousin, friend, or stranger brag on our behalf. It is undoubtedly a show of pride, happiness and love. That is not a bad thing, but a particularly good thing. Keep in mind that we have the same responsibility and are (per social norms) required to reciprocate the promotion of their achievements and accomplishments. We should take pride in their wins and celebrate them as our own. In the event that our community refuses to participate in the boastful celebrations of each other and promotes negative social feedback to those attempting to recognize themselves and/or other people for their success, we can always take time to quietly and diligently celebrate those wins. It can be as simple as a few encouraging words, a note, a gift, or a small gathering. These celebrations allow us to focus on the positive emotions that generate happier and healthier lifestyles.

Chapter Seven

BALANCE

THE

CORE

Relax!

We all need a way to reexamine, recenter and balance our core. Whether we choose to read an inspirational book, practice meditating, deliberately staying in bed a few moments longer, commuting with nature, praying, going to church, or participating in an activity specifically designed to fulfill our own need. It's healthy to ensure that we set aside time to relax, refocus and enjoy life. Things can get overwhelming at times and it's beneficial to have techniques in place that assist us in redirecting our energy into a positive direction. We're all capable of getting caught up in the hype of society, the stress, the burden, and the need to succeed. Sometimes it can become difficult to focus on the truly important things in life and the reasons we're strolling through our everyday mundane existence. It's always important to take the time we need to keep our focus and relax. In order to successfully achieve this it's important that we take the time to reexamine ourselves. To recenter our internal energy and/or spiritual force to emanate productively. When we look inward to understand our spiritual and emotional aspects of ourselves we're able to cultivate our inner light and help it radiate outward. Think about a battery and how it stores energy and converts it to electrical energy after some time the battery will stop working. A rechargeable battery, can be recharged and be used again. We exert ourselves and disperse energy.

Therefore, we need an opportunity to recharge our selves in order to continue to disperse energy. This applies to both the physical and spiritual aspects of our body. When we fail to pay attention to our own requirements it can lead to physical and emotional symptoms. In which, many individuals will turn to a physician for assistance. The unfortunate thing about modern medicine is that it can lead to a series of addictions. The pills being manufactured cause a synthetic release of hormones that allow people to feel relaxed and provide a false since of contentment. This is not a permanent resolution but a temporary relief, if prescribed over long periods of time, it can cause adverse reactions. People can become easily addicted to legal narcotics because they are so easily accessible via a script from their physician. However, the power to abstain from drugs is in the hands of each individual and we all have a choice to restrain ourselves. Knowledge goes a long way in understanding the best preventive outcome for a person's health and welfare. The best way to really overcome severe symptoms, most commonly anxiety, is to find a trustworthy doctor. In the event that someone may feel that their mental health is in jeopardy it is crucial that they find a doctor that can be trusted. What are signs of anxiety? Anxiety affects individuals in many different ways. It can start as an uneasy feeling in your stomach. It can progress into more severe symptoms. In some individuals the symptoms can become so severe that it mimics a heart attack. The symptoms are extremely broad and can include such things as: general worriment, phobias, panic attacks, and other signs of mental or physical disorders. Many of us have felt overwhelming symptoms at one time or another. However, if you feel repeated episodes, or feel that you are encountering severe anxiety symptoms, the best action is to visit a doctor. Find a doctor that is trustworthy. These are symptoms that should not only be treated with a pill. A good doctor would suggest and/or refer you to an anxiety coach or a specialist who can assist you with techniques and/or coping skills. Usually specific goals are constructed to align to an individual's specific need. The therapy an individual receives should be tailored specifically to that individual's symptoms and/or diagnosis. This ensures that the individual can overcome and manage their symptoms successfully. Hopefully, without becoming dependent on a synthetic drug because breaking an addiction can be difficult. And, more than likely someone who becomes addicted will still require treatment for the original symptom as well as addiction rehabilitation caused by prolong use of the prescribed narcotic. Knowledge and understanding goes a long way in overcoming most common human reactions. People experiencing overwhelming, excessive and persistent symptoms should feel confident in seeking assistance from professionals. Humans are social creatures by nature and sometimes people need the help of others to overcome difficulties. Therefore, when it comes to finding a doctor don't settle for someone based on a degree, or their eagerness to write a prescription because that can lead to disappointment. The way we're made to feel in the presence of another person makes a huge difference in the quality of the outcome of our own well being. We must keep ourselves in mind when making choices that will impact our personal lives. Therefore, ask the people around you for recommendations and don't hesitate to share your good experiences with others. We're all looking for a positive solution. Also keep in mind that not everyone who experiences anxiety needs to see a doctor. Anxiety is a natural reaction to stress. Simply finding ways to alleviate stress will do wonders in improving one's health.

GOALS?

Are you trying to find ways to relax more? Perhaps, you want to change your habits or learn ways to cope. There are many techniques available. You just have to find one that works for you. The first step is recognizing your goal. What is your goal?

Relieving stress

Building confidence

Increasing self-esteem

Losing weight

Breaking bad habits

Releasing creative blocks

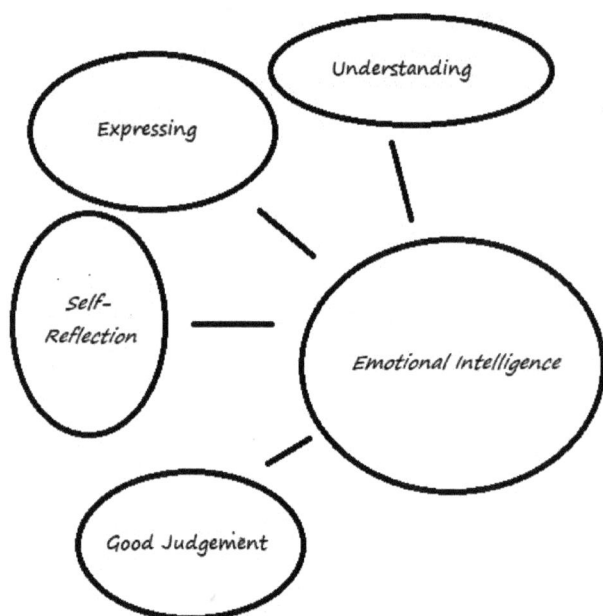

Emotional Intelligence:

Emotional intelligence is the ability to understand, control, and express our own emotions in a sympathetic manner using good judgment.

Most everyone has been introduced to the idea that humans are emotional creatures. Being able to understand our own emotions and how they play a role in the way we react to different stimuli provides us with a unique perception in understanding others more compassionately. It also enhances our own ability to maintain self control when we're confronted with stress. Emotional intelligence allows us to be more aware of ourselves and of other people. We can consciously increase our understanding of emotions in many ways, some include: observing and evaluating our own feelings, examining how we react to stressful situations, thinking of ways we could have handled a situation more appropriately, and ultimately becoming more self aware. By cultivating our own abilities we're providing ourselves ways to maintain self- control, learn from our mistakes, understand the importance of forgiving ourselves, and advancing our own motivation to move forward. Our emotions are real and in several ways science has proven them to be part of our humanness. There can be happiness found in our emotions and there can be sadness too. A variety of external and internal stimulants can trigger an assortment of feelings. More often than not people are emotional. Some people may proclaim they're not emotional and even describe emotions as a sensitive feature. However, majority of these people are not without emotions. Most of them are very much on the emotional side. They've just quantified their definition of emotions in a manner that prevents them from having to accept their truth. But, there is always a chance that the person proclaiming to be unemotional is an actual psychopath. However, a lot of people who regard themselves as non-emotional have been surrounded by people who love them, support them, and provided them with a sense of security that has allowed them to balance their emotions at an early age. So more than likely they have adopted learned behavior skills inattentively which does allow them to cope and overcome problems more efficiently. This is because during their lifetime someone has taught them how to redirect their emotions in a positive manner.

This could've been a parent, a spouse, a friend, or a mentor. So they're capable of instinctively responding to stressful stimuli more ideally than someone who hasn't been influenced with the same enlightenment. These people may consider themselves as a forth-right, candid, cut-to-the-chase type of personality but they're generally natural problem solvers capable of handling difficult situations productively and effectively. Where as, an individual without a trained mind adept in responding wisely to stressful situations who consider themselves a no-nonsense, matter-of-fact personality can cause havoc. Especially for those individuals who practice self-awareness and actively tries to pay attention to their present state of reality.

Because they have to bare witness to the chaotic

discord of emotional flurries gusting through the

atmosphere. The mistrust and faulting that's being

tossed around like a game of hot potatoes. The

individual proclaiming to have no emotional ties will

display a strong intensity of disappointment in the

inefficiencies of those around them. They don't appear

to take in consideration that they maybe causing a hail

storm of emotional down pour while they're

proclaiming that emotions roll off of them with no

personal affect. While everyone in their path is

scurrying to avoid them all together they're

proclaiming they can never get anyone to help them

when they need it. Not once taking heed to the idea

that they're emitting stress by denying their own

infliction. And, stress is a genuine adversary in the

internal conflict within us all. Our bodies perceive

stress as a threat. Once that happens the amygdala

triggers the fight or flight response which literally

hijacks the rational side of the brain because it

perceives it as a challenge. The amygdala takes over

and it's ready to react. During this time it will prevent

the rational side of the brain from having any input

over any response. That being the case the odds of

resolving anything in a positive manner with someone

in this state will be extremely low. Recognizing that

someone maybe in this state will allow us to control

our own distress feelings, ensure the individual doesn't

feel threatened and give them the room they need to calm down. There are some helpful pointers for us to remember and that would be to avoid raising our voice, avoid trying to argue our point (the logical area of the mind is shut down at this point), and avoid coming across as threatening in any manner and hopefully we can prevent triggering any unwanted responses. Once the individual is able to relax, they will be more open to communicate and interact on an appropriate level. The chemicals that are body releases and certain environmental factors are key components to the circumstance. There is no set time frame on how long this emotional state will last because it is a subconscious involuntary trigger. However, there are ways of developing a stronger defense and realigning

our perception that will allow the logical side of our

brain to maintain it's control longer in stressful

situations. By enhancing our awareness we increase

our likelihood to think rationally in stressful situations.

Through learned behavior skills and the

implementation of coping mechanisms we can

maintain our stress level response more reasonably.

Identifying thoughts and emotional patterns help us to

keep track of our own tendencies in order to contour

practices designed to help us maintain control. This

will assist us in managing our own reactions and

strengthen our ability to overcome stressful situations

more favorably.

USEFUL TECHNIQUES:

REFLECTIVE TECHNIQUES

These techniques are used to help an individual change a self-destructive behavior pattern and to improve the development of new traits that will aid them in overcoming problems more efficiently. The techniques are designed to encourage an individual to redirect their old habits and apply coping skill mechanisms that will help to strengthen other skills for instance information-processing skills. Reflective Therapy generally starts with a model of approximation for the purpose of comprehension and prediction. It influences a person's thoughts, feelings and behaviors towards reaching their intended goal. Strategies are created to change or strengthen the way an individual thinks, acts, or responds to allow the individual to overcome difficulties or obstacles that may arise. The goal of this technique is to realign old habits and boost happiness at the same time. This is done primarily by focusing on the solutions, challenging the way a person thinks, ultimately changing bad habits, and conforming self-destructive behavioral patterns into healthier habits. Who can benefit from this technique? People who tend to focus on the negative things and ignore the positive ones. People who have a tendency to jump to conclusions without any evidence at all. People who tend to blame others when things go wrong. Etc,. A great technique to start with would be to keep a journal (this allows a way to gather data by keeping track of moods, thoughts, feelings, and actions). Because, being aware of dysfunctional behavior patterns will make it easier to avert from the self-destructive ones.

VISUALIZATION TECHNIQUES

There are many different variations of visualization techniques available to assist a person reach their aspiration. The technique is basically a mental rehearsal technique that involves imagining what one is desiring and envisioning it as a reality. It evolves around the self-fulfilling prophecy theory. The idea of what one focuses on is what one will attract. The different types of techniques may include: mental contracting, law of attraction, and positive affirmation.

Someone would simply identify what it is they want and focus on achieving it. Then visualize themselves having it or possessing it. Simply concentrate on all of the positive benefits that will come from attaining it and stay away from any impeding thoughts. Because this technique definitely requires a person to set aside any doubt or uncertainties and maintain confidence in the outcome.

SELF-HYPNOSIS TECHNIQUES

These techniques usually focus around improving perception, balancing emotions, and providing a relaxed frame of mind. Most all hypnosis techniques are similar to meditation as it requires a quiet place with no distractions. Decide on a hypnosis goal (relaxing, loosing weight, getting a promotion). Clear the mind of any negative thoughts and worries that plague the mind. Imagine the tension throughout the body is relaxing. Focus on the feeling of inner peace and visualize that you are expelling tension and inhaling tranquility. Then take slow, deep breathes and visualize on the goal. Hopefully, an extremely relaxed feeling will emerge as the goal becomes the primary focus. This practice is known to increase the capacity for forgiveness, self-acceptance, relieving stress, and much more. It also helps to rid the mind of any negative thoughts and worries that may plague it. Some people find it helpful to incorporate three or four positive affirmations (I am happy, I am loved, I am successful, etc.,).

THESE TECHNIQUES ARE USED BY MANY PEOPLE TO ENHANCE AND IMPROVE MANY DIFFERENT ASPECTS OF THERE LIFE. COMMON GOALS MAY INCLUDE BUT ARE NOT LIMITED TO:

- BUILDING CONFIDENCE
- CHANGING BAD HABITS
- TREATING ADDICTIONS
- ALLEVIATING ANXIETY
- OVERCOMING DEPRESSION
- PROMOTING CREATIVITY
- SETTING GOALS
- INCREASING SELF ESTEEM
- SOLVING PROBLEMS
- RELIEVING STRESS
- MANAGING PAIN
- LOSING WEIGHT

TECHNIQUE:

Find a technique that works for you. There are plenty of techniques out there that consist of eating healthy, taking on hobbies, relaxation, physical fitness, meditation, and more...

RESPIRE:

Breathe, it is important to remember to take a deep breath. This increases the oxygen flow to your brain.

UNDERSTAND:

Being self-aware allows you the ability to recognize, accept and manage your emotions.

SURMISE:

Assume that something triggered the emotional response, such as: anger, stress, or fear. Theorize on what that might have been.

THINK:

Think of ways that your response can be more suitable in the future.

&

Learn:

Acquire self-knowledge to ensure the best self-management options to fit your needs.

Overcome:

The best way to overcome a primal response is to put your techniques into practice. There is no quick fix surrounding human emotions. Only the ability to heighten knowledge and manage emotions to the best of your abilities.

Voice:

Don't be afraid to apologize for over reacting. Share your experience with others because this may help you to relate and empathize.

Effectiveness:

Once you notice that you are NOT over reacting to an internal or external stimuli that normally would cause a negative-response, you know that your technique is effective.

Chapter Eight

OPTIMISTIC

VIEW

OF

LIFE

Encouragement!

It is sometimes challenging and difficult to keep a positive outlook when we are struggling through hard times. During these difficult times, there are ways in which we can self-motivate. Yes, we can motivate ourselves and others to move forward and maintain a positive outlook. We all face hard times, failures or difficulties at some point in our lives. It is the way we view these trying times that determine how much of an impact that we allow them to have on our lives. Our minds operate on a subconscious level that impacts our moods, perceptions, and behaviors. Being mindful of the situations happening around us, maintaining a positive outlook, and encouraging others to focus on the bright side of things will allow for a more positive outcome. Using positive words help to produce oxytocin, the neurochemical that helps trigger positive feelings. Have you ever been watching a movie and seen someone in a car that is listening to an audio cassette or compact disc and they are repeating the words from the audio out loud. The messages are normally positive affirmations, such as: I can do this..., I am successful..., I am great..., etc., This is because the words we hear impact our perception of the world and how we view it. Encouraging and optimistic expression influence us to remain optimistic and positive. Our minds listen to everything we say externally and internally. The inspiring phrases that we hear help to keep us focused and optimistic. In return this gives us an advantage in dealing with the difficult situations that we are presented with in life and provide us the ability to carry on enjoying life. There are many places to find inspiring and motivating words of encouragement. It takes very little time to read an inspirational or motivation quote each day. Some people find solace in reading bible verses. Some people like to set aside time each morning or night to read one chapter in an inspirational or motivational book. Some prefer positive affirmations on video or compact disc devices. Some people pick through the morning news paper articles and read only the articles that focus on the positive things going on in their community. In today's society with immediate access to social media and the internet there is an abundance of positive sources easily available. You are in charge of what you allow into your bubble of happiness.

We should strive for a happy and joyous life even when things don't appear to be going well. We create and generate our own happiness around the things in life that we encounter.

When I make mistakes I like to blurt out, "I make a mess that is what I do best." It prevents me from getting frustrated with myself and it replaces the disappointment with merriment.

THE PEARLS OF WISDOM

A MOTIVATIONAL VARIETY TO INFLUENCE

A POSITIVE OUTLOOK:

Focus on what you have that way you are not worrying about what you don't have.

Don't dive into despair when it's cold out.

Never lose hope because even a faint light becomes brighter as it darkens.

We can complain about the grass being high, or value the ground for being fertile.

Perfectionism is nothing more than idolism because no human is without fault.

An uninformed man is unaware that he is ignorant, but an informed man knows he is ignorant.

Tomorrow brings a new dawn, a new dawn brings a new beginning, and a new beginning brings a new rise.

We have exited the past so pay attention to the present.

Persistence is the remedy to failure.

Necessities are the root of happiness and everything branches from there.

Surrender your hate and liberate your heart.

Forsake not your own heart by holding a grudge for another.

Learn to forgo the bitterness of hatred by renouncing resentment.

Assumptions have a tendency to evolve into regrets.

Hatred never lays dormant. It festers and poisons the soul. You would need to secrete the bile to cure the heart.

To fully apprehend our apprehension, we must deliberate with our consciousness within.

One who fills their mind with knowledge but forgets to fill their heart with love can never feel fulfilled.

It's true that suffering can bring sorrow, but it can also inspire evolution.

Before someone can truly understand oneself they must first become acquainted with themselves.

Righteousness is a state of mind in which everyone attempts to justify. However, kindness is an action in which everyone should attempt to maintain.

Interpretations can alter clarification when things are misunderstood.

Everyone is created to be specifically unique. A puzzle can't be whole without many different pieces and every single piece has a purpose. Therefore, it's important to accept that everyone is made specifically remarkable for a reason and it's because of those distinctions we succeed.

Don't get caught in the redundancy of simply existing because it can prevent you from learning how to live.

To find tranquility seek nature.

It's almost impossible to do anything without learning something. Therefore, as long as you try you will always learn.

It takes courage to do what your passionate about without worrying about what other people think.

Don't cut someone off at the knees to make yourself appear important.

You can't expect others to trust in your abilities when you're not willing to trust in theirs.

Since our eyes are on the outside of our face it's easy to assume that we should look outside of ourselves to seek answers. But, the truth is that those who've learned to look within themselves are the one's that have truly found enlightenment.

Chapter Nine

CONSTRUCT

ALLIANCES

WITH

OTHERS

Relationships!

Having trust or faith in someone is vital to building an authentic relationship. When we trust someone it allows us to engage more willingly with them. Trust is a key component in building a strong intimate relationship with family, friends, and lovers. It allows us to unveil our true selves without fear of judgment. We can freely share all of our flaws and insecurities. This allows us to create a stronger relationship bond. But, in today's modern world trusting someone can be a terrifying concept. This is mainly because it requires us to expose ourselves to a certain amount of vulnerability. The uncertainty that goes along with trusting someone can be very frightening and it causes many people to become apprehensive about who they trust. Therefore, it's not unusual to hear someone say, "I don't trust them." Most people don't realize the true impact of the statement. When you here someone say, "I don't trust them" usually the individual is merely trying to express their uncertainty about the individual, but this statement is actually a complaint of wrongdoing against the individual. In making the claim, the accuser is exonerating themselves from any responsibilities that may transpire that requires them to place trust or faith in that person. This prevents any positive progression towards building a relationship between them. There is not much the other party can do to overcome this judgment. They have already been placed on the defensive side of the assertion which implies that they are untrustworthy. But, trust can be directed towards the good qualities that someone possess, it doesn't have to be an all or nothing circumstance. Example: I asked John to build a house for me. John is not a carpenter or contractor. My trust in John is misguided. However, if I ask John to repair my internet connection and he is an internet technician than my trust in John is true. John can probably tackle the task successfully. Therefore, I may not be able to trust that John can build me a house, but I can trust that John will repair my internet. Our own understanding and awareness is the key to truly understanding others. Often times we may subconsciously influence what we believe to be true over what is actually true. We may

react based upon our own insecurities and fears. It's

not uncommon for an individual to play out

possibilities in their own mind. Then, project those

insecurities onto someone else. In the event that we

find ourselves mistrusting someone, we can take the

time to ask ourselves, "why?" Is there something

specific they have or have not done to make us feel this

way? Is there anything that they can do to help us

rebuild that trust? Sometimes, it is simply our own

conception based upon an unfavorable or painful

feeling surrounding a past event that has placed us at a

disadvantage. Especially, when it comes to trusting

someone. It is not always the fault of the person,

themselves, that we are projecting the mistrust onto. What if the situation is reversed and someone doesn't trust us? How can we overcome this judgment against us? We can take a moment and try to remember if there is anything we may have done that could have undermined someone's trust in us. We can ask them if we are not aware of anything. We can confirm our desire and willingness to restore that trust. We can try to convince them that they're wrong. However, we probably will not be able to persuade them that their judgment is wrong. Most of the time it is better to be the progressive party and apologize, even if we feel that their judgment is one-sided. There are many things that we could probably justify, or have a reasonable explanation for happening. However, trying to convince someone that they maybe acting a little judgmental or short sighted could bring about further discord. Therefore, we can be the bigger person and try to regain their trust. Hopefully, the effort we put forth will give rise to a positive outcome. In the event that we have tried our best to regain their trust and we're still unable to prevail, we can simply move on with our lives. Unfortunately, criticism is a part of reality and we all hold different opinions. We can take assurance in the fact that we did make a vigorous attempt to rebuild their trust. Perhaps, there isn't anything else we can do. But, We can accept that we tried and move on with our own lives. Can we have a relationship without trust? Yes, trust provides us with stronger, intimate relationships. But, relationships come in many forms. One commonality in all healthy relationships is the willingness to accept others for who they are as an individual and not who we want them to be. That doesn't mean to stop encouraging them to become their ideal-selves as we strive to be our true selves. It simply implies truly accepting them for who they are. Elsie would say that you should always look for the good in everyone. She leads with guidance, encouragement, and unconditional love. She does not use intimidation, force or fear to get her point across. The belief that she has in people is admirable. I can still recall one early morning as Elsie approached a bus stop in her car, she noticed two young adolescent children about to fight. There were already many other children and adults standing around watching. But, no one was taking action to defuse the situation. Therefore, she got out of her vehicle, walked over and stood between both children. She did not know either child. She looked at both of the children and expressed her concerns about their behavior. She emphasized on the fact that their own parents would be disappointed if they could see them behaving in such a manner. She conveyed her hope that they would apologize to each other and go home. Both of the children listened. They went their separate ways and the situation was defused. Some of the other adults approached her wanting to know why she was not scared. The children had knifes and she could have gotten stabbed. Her reply was simple, "I seen two scared kids in over their heads and neither one appeared threatening to me." Her faith in general is absolutely radiant. The manner in which she can see past someone's emotional distress and maintain belief in them is astonishing. I am definitely biased based on the love I have for Elsie. But, I would define her as a saint that walks the earth. There are many courageous, inspiring women and men that are present in this world. Their presence alone inspires love, gratefulness, acceptance, forgiveness and faith. They exhale it like a breath. They have the ability to maintain faith in people even when other people may view them as hopeless. They do not project themselves as being with out flaw or fault. But, their actions encourage others to strive harder to look for the good in the people around them. They are the living embodiment of the phrase, "Live by example." Whereas, a lot of us quantify our acceptance of others based on our sense of trust. They simply accept the belief that people are good and worth trusting. What is "trust?" It is an unyielding belief in a person or thing. Therefore, how can we have trust in someone that we don't actually know? In actual reality we are placing a prejudgment upon them. However, if we search for a synonym of "trust," we'll probably see the word "belief." This is because the two terms, "trust" and "belief," are classified as being similar to one another. What is belief? It's an acceptance that something is the case or that some statement about the existence is true. Therefore, we can believe in someone even when we don't have trust in them. How does that work? I asked my friend, Jack, to repair my car. I believe that he will repair my car because he is a mechanic but I don't trust that Jack will have it done by the weekend because I know Jack likes to procrastinate. Therefore, I have faith that he will get it done as soon as he can. Should I be angry because he told me that he would try to have it done by Tuesday. After, I told him I needed it done by Monday? Especially, since I seen him at a gathering on Saturday. No, I should remain grateful to Jack because he agreed to repair my car in the first place. I might feel a little disappointed in Jack for not making the car a priority. But, I still have to remember that he is setting aside his time to repair my car because he is my friend. He is still using his time and talent to help me. The fact that my car stopped working is not his fault. Nor, is it his responsibility to repair it. My expectations should not over shadow the fact that Jack is using his time. The time he could be spending doing something other than repairing my car. The fact that I need my car working by that following Monday in order to fulfill my own obligation is not Jack's burden. I can choose to have someone else do the work. It does not over shadow the support Jack is extending to

157

me by repairing my car (regardless of how long the task may take). He is repairing my car to help me. The fact that he doesn't want to put his life on hold to repair it in the time restraints that I require or need does not nullify the reality that Jack is still accommodating me by agreeing to repair my car. He's doing it out of the kindness of his heart. Therefore, is it fair for me to repay Jack's kindness by saying, "I missed my commitment because Jack did not repair my car over the weekend, and I know he really was not doing anything" or "I would have made my commitment, if Jack wasn't fraternizing and spent all his time hobnobbing instead of repairing my car?" Unfortunately, this type of perception seems to circulate among many individuals and this conception does not help coalesce strong relationships. I should be grateful to him that he took his time to fix my car. I should also reciprocate the favor if Jack needs assistance and I have the ability or capability to assist. In the event that I am truly unable to assist with his concern, I should empathize with his hardship and let him know that if there is anything I am able or capable of assisting him with than I am ready and willing. Some individual's will come up with an excuse such as: Jack didn't repair my car in time for me to keep my appointment, therefore, I don't see any reason that I should be concerned about his problem now. This does not fall into the "law of reciprocity." It can also have an adverse reaction towards the person that takes this stance because the people around them may begin to view them as an ungrateful person. This may eventually lead to the people in their lives avoiding them. They may become reluctant to provide assistance to them based on their inability to appreciate others. But, another example (making this one simple): Sally asked to barrow my reading book. But, I know her dogs have destroyed most of her books. I don't trust that she will return it without any damage because her dogs like to chew on books. Therefore, if I loan her the book it is an act of faith that she will return the book without any damage. I would need to place faith in Sally to overcome my own fear that her dogs will destroy my book. The truth is that the term, "trust" has become an idolization surrounding relationships. Not all relationships require trust. Once someone is emotionally hurt, they can develop a fear of being hurt. It becomes harder for them to trust other people. They may draw back from building relationships in general and place a metaphorical wall between themselves and others. Their behavior may appear more defiant, difficult, and oppositional. This conduct is usually an involuntary response to conceal their hurt and protect themselves from further emotional pain. They have a hard time trusting people and that is where "faith" takes over. They can have faith in a person and at the same time mistrust their motives. It is okay to be

161

cautious of whom you place your trust in. But, we need to keep faith in each other in order to maintain good relationships. It is important to accept people for who they are, but, that doesn't mean you are obligated to share your secrets with them. You can try to understand them because this will help bridge a connection. Why do we need to form relationships with other people? It helps maintain social structures that support our emotional well-being and survival. Mutual respect and fair exchange are expected in social reciprocity. The balance of social interaction begins with politeness. We return favors and cooperate. We try hard to follow the golden rule and the interdependency of a good relationship requires both parties to contribute. Reciprocal respect is not possible if both parties are not being respectful. The failure to reciprocate can cause a negative social interaction. Negative reciprocity normally occurs when one party is being disrespected or not being considered. Those that fail to reciprocate do so at their own peril. It can destroy the individuals social standing in a group or community. This is a demonstration of a self- destructive behavior that has the ability to end even a strong relationship. The way we treat others has a real consequence on the nature of our being. Social reciprocity is a form of interaction in which we accept the kind actions of others with appreciation and we respond with a kind response. This is the foundation to a lasting relationship. Why are relationships important? The interconnections we construct with other human beings provide us with a sense of belonging. Which instinctively reduces negative thoughts while invoking the essential motivation to embrace the joy and simplicity of life.

Chapter Ten

POEMS

ABOUT

KNOWING

ELSIE...

ANGEL SPIRIT

Angel Spirit, shining bright,
In a secular world of delight.
Being born unto you,
Was a blessing in my sight.

What heavenly realm?
What kingdom in the sky,
Constructed a gem like you?
One that forever seems to shine.

A steady beam of brightness;
Always illuminating this sphere.
The earthly world seems heavenly,
Every time you are near.

What creator? What deity?
What goddess placed you here?
To irradiate such brightness,
So impeccably far and near.

Divinely delivered unto you,
A fulfillment to your devotion.
The benevolence of your being,
It's an honor to have been chosen.

BECAUSE OF YOU...

The acceptance of your being.
The tenderness of your heart.
The gentleness of your hand.
And, the humbleness of your smarts.

With the love that your heart provided.
With the loyalty in which you pledged.
With the guidance that you bestowed.
And, through the wisdom that you shared.

You have taught me to love.
You have taught me to bond.
You have taught me to overcome.
And, you have taught me to forgive.

You've lead me with a heart.
You've lead me with a way.
You've lead me with a vision.
And, you've lead me for a reason.

Now, I can feel using my heart.
Now, I can act using my faith.
Now, I can see using my sight.
And, promptly rationalize using my brain.

It's because or your love,
I see the world fondly.
It's because of your loyalty,
I see the world adventurously.
It's because of your guidance,
I see the world encouragingly.
And, it's because of your wisdom,
I'm forever grateful to live life graciously.

ELSIE

There can be no other exactly like her.
She's rare, unique, and second to none.
She's precious, invaluable, and...
God only made one.

No riches or silver could buy this treasure.
Her value is just way too high.
She's a gem. She's an angel.
She is one of a kind.

She's adored and cherished with admirable esteem.
She's loved, regarded, and revered.
My affection for her, I hold so dear.
For the love I have harbors no fear.

We all try to acclaim her as our own.
But, she belongs to the holy one.
Oh. How generous is he to share?
To have chosen me to be placed in her care.

THE WAY SHE SHARES...

Her faith is so abundant.
It excretes from every pore.
You can't help but notice.
Especially, as it pours.

Her belief is so profuse.
It emanates from her smile.
There is no suppressing it.
It spreads way too wild.

Her optimism is so effusive.
It goes gusting through the wind.
There is no controlling it.
The movement has no end.

Her love is so radiant.
You can feel the glow.
There is no denying it.
The flame steady grows.

Her presence is so illuminating.
That's the warmth she shares.
There is no way to fight it.
The kindness is always there.

Notes:

Notes:

172

Notes:

ABOUT THE AUTHOR

Michele Campbell was born in Charleston, South Carolina. She was the youngest of her siblings and she is eternally grateful for the love and support that her family provided to her throughout her life. She married into the Campbell family. The pride that the Campbell's hold for their ancestry is phenomenal. One of her favorite past holidays/vacations was a trip that she took, with her husband, to visit *The Campbell Castle*. She has worked for some of the largest communication companies in the world, but she doesn't allow any job to define her. She will quickly admit that being a mother is the most important and gratifying position of her life. She loves her children unconditionally. Writing a book has always been on her "bucket-list" of things to accomplish and she has achieved this spectacularly in her "must-read" inspirational, Knowing Elsie...

www.ingramcontent.com/pod-product-compliance
Lightning Source LLC
Chambersburg PA
CBHW071855020426
42331CB00010B/2524